Written by Melissa Snowden
Designed by Michelle Martinez

Copyright © 2012 Scholastic Inc.

Tangerine Press
an imprint of
SCHOLASTIC
www.scholastic.com

Scholastic and Tangerine Press and associated logos are trademarks and/or registered trademarks of Scholastic Inc.

Published by Tangerine Press, an imprint of Scholastic Inc.,
557 Broadway, New York, NY 10012

10 9 8 7 6 5 4 3 2 1

ISBN: 978-0-545-46186-3

Printed and bound in Jiaxing, China

Scholastic Canada Ltd.; Markham, Ontario
Scholastic Australia Pty. Ltd; Gosford, NSW
Scholastic New Zealand Ltd.; Greenmount, Auckland

Photo credits: © 2012: Ardea : 73 N, 17 (Jean Miche Labat), 73 J (John Daniels); Artville Stock/Animal Attitude: Tab4, 39; Dreamstime/Kelly Richardson: 23; Getty Images: 73 M (Dave King), 36 (Debra Cohn-Orbach), cover (GK Hart/Vikki Hart/Brand X Pictures), 32 (Radius Images/PhotoLibrary); iStockphoto: 10, 13 (101 cats), 16 (andipantz), 45 (Andrey_Kuzmin), 69 (Anna Furman), 57 (bigworld), 50 (Dixi_), 60 (foment), 15 (frenc), 48 (GlobalP), 11 (HannamariaH), 34 (jsheets19), 12 (kavu), 22 (kuban_girl), 53 (LeventKonuk), 43 (linncurrie), 19 (Luso), 64, 70 (Marco Neumayr), 52 (mashabuba), 7 (Tatjana Romanova), 59 (Tina_Rencelj), 14 (winhorse), 56 (yykkaa); Kimball Stock/ Ron Kimballk : 24, 25; Leanne Thomas: 37, 73; Photos.com: Tab5 (Eric Isselée), 73 K (Francesco Carta); Professional Photography Library: Dogs & Cats: 9 top, 9 bottom, 73 I, 73 P; Shutterstock, Inc.: 28 (Antonín Vodák), 73 L (Kapu), 20 (kuban_girl), 29 (Linn Currie), 54 (Lusoimages), 19 (MAErtek), 30 (Red-Blue Photo), 58 (Tony Campbell), 1 (Utekhina Anna), 38 (Utekhina Anna), 2, 3 (vita khorzhevska), 9 center, 46 (Vitaly Titov & Maria Sidelnikova), 73 top (WilleeCole).

You Look Mar-velous!

Your cat is one of your best friends! Kitty makes you smile when it does silly things. He or she is glad to see you when you get home and follows you wherever you go. Playtime is fun when your kitty's up for it. And most importantly, your cat is always there for you.

Your cat likes to be pampered, just like people. You know kitty's favorite meal, when it's playful, and what kind of toys your furry friend likes best. Giving your kitten some extra love with home-made treats and gifts can really make him or her feel like royalty.

It just takes a bit of creativity and a whole lot of love! In this book, you'll find simple and fun (and useful!) goodies for your favorite feline. Are you ready for a purr-fectly good time? Let's get your kitty's style on!

What's Your Kitty Style?

Everyone (and every cat!) is unique in his or her own way. What kind of cat style do you have? Take this quiz to find out! Get to know which kitty you most resemble.

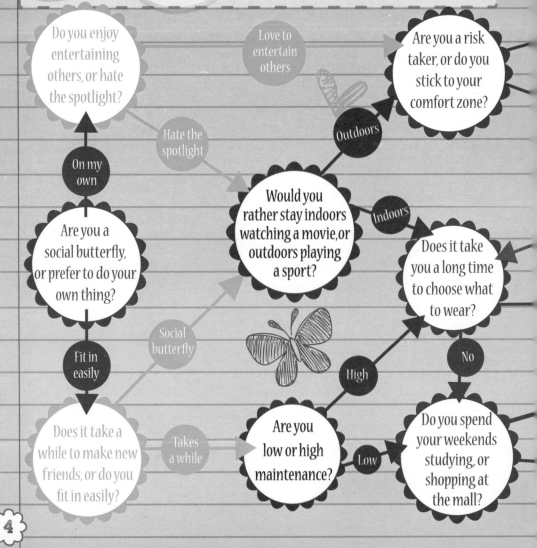

Do you enjoy entertaining others, or hate the spotlight?

Love to entertain others

Are you a risk taker, or do you stick to your comfort zone?

Hate the spotlight

On my own

Outdoors

Are you a social butterfly, or prefer to do your own thing?

Would you rather stay indoors watching a movie, or outdoors playing a sport?

Indoors

Does it take you a long time to choose what to wear?

Fit in easily

Social butterfly

High

No

Does it take a while to make new friends, or do you fit in easily?

Takes a while

Are you low or high maintenance?

Low

Do you spend your weekends studying, or shopping at the mall?

4

Risk taker

Do you act like a class clown, or would you rather sit at the front of the class?

Comfort zone

Do you have a few best buds, or a lot of acquaintances?

Best buds

In the fashion world, would you rather model, design clothing, or do everyone's hair and makeup?

Yes

Acquaintances

No

Yes

Do you get bored easily?

Studying

Really don't like to get my hair wet

Shopping

Do you like swimming, or would you rather stay out of the water?

Love the water

Are you more soft-spoken, or would you rather be on stage?

Quiz Results

Class clown →

Wild Child!

You go with your gut instinct and create your own trends, even if it means bold, outrageous color combos and patterns. Try animal prints mixed with bright solids. You are most like an Abyssinian.

Design clothes →

Hair and makeup →

Busy Bee!

You like to stay on your toes. Your busy schedule means you have a lot of friends, but not a lot of time. Keep it simple with solid colors, sneakers, and cute, sporty outfits. You are most like a Siamese.

Model →

Posh!

So posh! You like to go glam and be the center of attention. You feel comfortable being dramatic, so try lots of flashy, studded accessories. You are most like a Persian.

Loud and proud on stage →

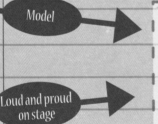

Cool Cat!

You are down-to-earth. You like to keep calm and keep it real. You do best in warm, natural colors with a laid-back style. You are most like a Ragdoll.

Soft-spoken and shy →

All Cats, Big and Small

Cats come in many shapes and sizes, big and small, all over the world. House cats (just like yours) are some of the best pets. For thousands of years, people have lived with their furry felines for many great reasons:

- ⭐ Ancient Egyptians kept cats for scaring away rats and other pests from their food storages.

- ⭐ Cats were so important to Ancient Egyptians that they soon came to be sacredly worshipped creatures (called "miws").

- ⭐ Greeks exported many of Egypt's domestic cats to deal with their own rodent infestations!

- ⭐ They were given as noble gifts to Chinese emperors, until commoners could finally own them.

- ⭐ People who traveled on ships also brought cats along because they hunted down mice.

- ⭐ The Pilgrims brought the first cats to the U.S.

- ⭐ During the 1800s, Victorians began entering their tamed kitties into cat shows.

Your Kitty Looks Gorgeous

So now you know, cats come in all shapes and sizes. And each cat looks unique on the outside, too! It's important to know this so you can properly dress and accessorize your furry friend. Take a look at some of these colors and patterns to find out your cat's marking style. Just remember, each cat is one-of-a-kind!

KITTY COLOR COMBOS

Colors	Pattern	Description
🐾 Black 🐾 Blue-gray 🐾 Brown 🐾 Cream	Solid or smoky	One main color throughout
🐾 Ginger 🐾 Gray 🐾 Orange	Tabby	Swirls, spots, or stripes
	Calico, patched tabby, and torties	Mitted or van
🐾 Silver 🐾 White	White markings	Bi-color or harlequin

Hair Lengths

Shorthaired cats come from all over the world, so even though they have similar fur length, their appearances are different from continent to continent. It's usual for shorthairs to have a variety of colorings, like tabby, calico, or solid.

Medium-haired cats have double-coated, thick fur. They come from a long line of mixing breeds, so you can find them in all colors, including solids, tabbies, and patched tabbies.

Longhaired cats also come with a variety of colors and markings. Many people decide to keep longhairs as pets because of their beautiful fur, which can grow up to 10 times as long as short-haired coats.

What's New Pussycat?

Your kitty has the life of luxury, and now she needs the wardrobe to go with it. This section will show you how to give your special friend a fashionable flair.

You definitely want kitty to look her best, but remember, if it's not comfortable, kitty won't like wearing it! Dressing her up in loose-fitting outfits or accessories is best, and anything that's easy to detach is even better. Keep in mind, if she wants to get out of her couture creation (for a bathroom break!), it'll need to be easy to remove!

Cute Kitty Collar

A collar is a must-have for your cat, but a plain one just won't do. Dazzle her up by making her a unique collar, accessorized with rhinestones and bows.

What you need:

- Fabric or nylon collar
- Nontoxic fabric paint
- Nontoxic fabric glue
- Rhinestones, beads, bows, or ribbons
- Grownup helper

What you do:

1. Decorate a fabric or nylon collar with craft or fabric paint.

2. Ask your grownup helper to help you add rhinestones or beads.

3. Secure them to the collar with fabric glue.

4. Tie bows or ribbons to the collar.

5. Let the glue dry before dressing your kitty in the new collar.

   Overnight is best!

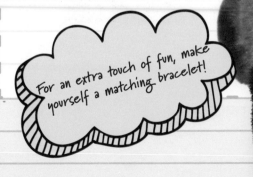

For an extra touch of fun, make yourself a matching bracelet!

Best Friend Bandanas

BFF

Try making this neck bandana for your kitty! Pick a color or pattern that suits your cat's personality. (Is she super girly? Try hot pink. Or is she a wild child? Go with a tiger or leopard print.) To make her even more kittylicious, find fabric with cat prints, paws, or yummy-looking fish on it.

What you need:

- ❖ Nontoxic fabric glue
- ❖ Pinking shears
- ❖ Ruler
- ❖ Iron
- ❖ Cotton fabric with cute pattern

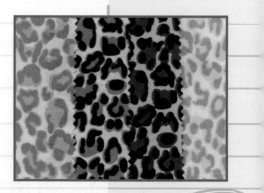

What you do:

1. Use the ruler to measure 12-14 square inches (30-36 cm) of fabric.

2. Cut into a square shape. Fold square diagonally, so that it's now a triangle.

3. With an adult helper, iron the folded triangle so that it's perfectly flat.

4. Apply fabric glue to the edges so they don't fray. (This works best with a craft paintbrush or an applicator tip.)

5. Do the same steps with another square of fabric, but make this one 20 square inches (51 cm) instead. This one will be for you!

6. Let glue on bandanna dry before dressing on you or your kitty.

7. Voilà! Now you and kitty have matching bandanas. You are both ready to rock out in style.

Classy
Cat Tuxedo

Got a special event coming up—a royal ball or wedding? If your handsome male cat needs to be a special guest, make this elegant tuxedo for him.

17

What you need:

- ❖ Nontoxic fabric glue
- ❖ Cotton fabric (white or black)
- ❖ Scissors
- ❖ Ruler
- ❖ Velcro
- ❖ Small bowtie (black, red, or patterned)
- ❖ 3 white buttons (optional)
- ❖ Nontoxic fabric marker (gray)

Velcro is one way to make any accessories or outfits for your cat easy to take off if he or she gets uncomfortable or needs a quick potty break.

What you do:

1. Measure a length of 5-7 inches (13-18 cm) (depending on the size of your kitty) of white fabric, 3 inches (8 cm) wide.

2. Cut fabric into rounded oval shape, making one of the shorter ends flat toward the edge.

3. If any of the edges are frayed, smooth their edges by gluing to the back. If you have three white buttons, glue them down the center of the fabric so they look like the buttons of a blouse. Otherwise, use a thin gray fabric marker to draw real-looking buttons down the center.

4. Use the fabric marker to draw very thin pleats straight down the fabric. They should look like six soft lines going straight down the shirt. Make sure that two of them are on either side of the buttons.

5. Cut a long strip of fabric, about 8 inches (20 cm) long to make the shirt collar. Measure the length around your kitty's neck so that you can adjust how long it should be. (You MUST make sure that it fits loosely around his neck, not tight!) Cut to fit.

6. Using fabric glue, glue pieces of Velcro to the ends of the fabric collar. Make sure that they attach together before you glue them permanently.

7. Glue the straight edge of the rounded "blouse" to the collar strip so that it hangs down the middle.

8. Glue the small bowtie to the collar center, at the top of the "blouse"; place it above the first button. (Make sure that you glue the bowtie very well—you don't want it to fall off!)

9. Leave flat to dry.

A Bride's Big Day

If it's your cat's wedding day, make her a special outfit to go with the tuxedo! Here are some steps to make a simple, but sparkly, veil for your kitty bride.

What you need:

- Tulle fabric (white or pink)
- Scissors
- Ribbon (white or pink)
- Rhinestones or flower decorations (optional)
- Nontoxic fabric glue (optional)

What you do:

1. Take a piece of ribbon and measure around your cat's neck for correct length. (The ribbon must fit loosely around her neck, not tight.) Cut to size.

2. Measure out and cut a piece of tulle fabric 9 x 6 inches (23 x 15 cm).

3. About 3 inches (7.5 cm) down from the top edge of the tulle, use scissors to lightly make very small holes in the tulle. Each tiny hole should be nearly 1 inch (2.5 cm) apart.

4. Weave the ribbon in and out of the tiny holes, and then scrunch the fabric together at the ribbon. (This will make the fabric look like a fluffy veil.)

5. If you have decorative rhinestones or small fabric flowers, you can use fabric glue to attach them to the outside of the veil. Allow them to dry.

Gently tie the ribbon veil around kitty's neck so that the long part of the veil hangs over her back. Now your beautiful bride-to-be is ready to go in style!

Say Cheese!

Beautiful Ballerina

Your kitty walks as light as a feather, sometimes just like a little ballerina! Once in this cute cat tutu, she'll seem like she's dancing on air.

What you need:

- 🐾 Tulle (any color)
- 🐾 Wide ribbon
- 🐾 Nontoxic fabric glue
- 🐾 Velcro
- 🐾 Scissors

Did you know that cats walk on their toes? That's why they seem so graceful. In ballet, a move called *pas de chat* translates to "cat step" where a ballerina leaps to the side. No wonder they are so light on their feet!

What you do:

1. Measure the ribbon around kitty's waist. (Make sure that it fits loosely, not too tight.)

2. Cut to size. Cut a piece of tulle (about 6 inches (15 cm) long). Gather it in the middle, pinching it with your fingers.

3. Take the pinched tulle and create a slipknot around the ribbon, so that it knots tightly to the ribbon.

4. Repeat Steps 2-3 with more pieces of tulle. Don't gather them around the entire ribbon, or else kitty might find it hard to walk if the skirt falls under her belly. (Instead, put enough tulle so that the skirt comes out of her back and sides.)

5. When satisfied with the amount of tulle, lay the skirt flat and use fabric glue to attach two pieces of Velcro to each end of the ribbon.

Once the Velcro has dried, fit the tutu around kitty's waist. And presto! Your diva cat is now a prima ballerina! For added effect, tie some ribbon around your cat's two front legs!

Whimsical Wand

Not only will this magical-looking wand make a fun toy for kitty, it will be a great accessory to her couture collection!

Use any color of felt or ribbons you'd like, or for a special treat, match them to your cat's outfit. If your cat likes to clown around, a bunch of bright colors might be really fun, or if she's very elegant, purples and reds would suit her best.

What you need:

- ❧ Nontoxic glue (optional)
- ❧ Duct tape
- ❧ Fishing line
- ❧ Felt fabric
- ❧ Wooden dowel
- ❧ Scissors

What you do:

1. Cut a piece of fishing line, about 12 inches (30.5 cm) long.

2. Cut 10 felt strips into various lengths. (The lines don't have to be straight.) Set aside one strip. Use the end of the fishing line to tie the ends of the strips together. Knot the fishing string around them very tight, tying it a few times.

3. With the extra strip of fabric you cut, tie around the knotted fishing line so that it also holds the fabric strips together. (You want to make sure that the fishing line doesn't slip out.)

4. Use duct tape to secure the fishing line and fabric strip to the end of the dowel. Wrap around many times to make sure it's tight. (It's best to tape over the fishing line more than once. For extra security, you can use nontoxic glue to hold down the fishing line and fabric.) Roll as much duct tape as you need!

5. On the opposite side of the stick, you can add duct tape so that it creates a grip for your hand. This might make it more comfortable to hold.

All right, now you and kitty are ready to play with her new colorful wand! Have fun!

Pampering Kitty

Your kitty really deserves the best in life. She has a one-of-a-kind personality, so she should have the life-style to match! Every kitten deserves to be pampered. This section is full of creative ideas for you to make for your feline friend! After all, handmade gifts are the most couture of all!

Decorate a Kitty Carrier

Be sure to ask a parent about decorating before you start! Make sure that it's okay to turn it into a work of art first!

A cat carrier is an essential item to have when owning a cat. But most don't appear unique or colorful at all— and probably do not match your cat's personality.

Here are some quick tips for decorating your cat's style:

❀ Stick on stickers! The more, the merrier, as you can stick on ones of all sizes, colors, and images.

❀ If your cat has a crush on Puss in Boots, add on some of those stickers. Or if kitty has a multidimensional personality, find some 3-D stickers shaped like different animals.

❀ Spell out your kitty's name with stencils. Using permanent markers, stencil the name of your cat onto her cat carrier in different colors.

❀ Glue decorations like rhinestones, bows, feathers, yarn, or soft boas onto the sides of the carrier. (Be sure to use nontoxic glue, or ask an adult to help you apply them with a hot glue gun.) Write some funny phrases.

❀ Use permanent markers to spell out some fun messages on your cat's carrier, or to do some cute graffiti. Make your pet taxi look like a real taxi by drawing in checkered boxes along the side! Or draw door handles to make it look like a traveling car, or add wheels so that it looks like a bus.

Use the carrier as a canvas to draw portraits of your kitty doing her favorite things around the house.

Decorate Bowls

Give your furry friend decorative bowls!

All you need is a food bowl and water bowl (plastic or ceramic work best) and dimensional paint. On the outside of the bowls, draw some cute pictures and clever messages for your cat! Decorate with cat paws, hearts, a crown, and your kitty's name (or whatever other cute things your cat would love) to make feeding time special. Then, let the paint dry for at least 24 hours before touching the paint or feeding your cat with them.

WARNING:
Do not decorate the inside of the bowl.

Sometimes cats come across as very fussy eaters. But did you know that some cats can have allergic reactions to plastic? If your kitty doesn't eat, she may be telling you that she doesn't like the food—but there's a chance that she's not happy with the bowl. Stainless steel and ceramic bowls are the best options for cats. They want to eat out of clean bowls, so rinse out dry food bowls daily. If the bowl is used with wet food, make sure to wash it thoroughly each day.

Feline-Friendly Placemat

When it's dinnertime, your kitty needs a special place to eat his food. By making him his very own "placemat," he will feel like he's right at home with your family ... even if he can't eat on the dinner table!

These are just a few ideas to inspire your creativity!

Start with a rectangular sheet of construction paper. Then add:

- ❖ Glitter glue
- ❖ Fabric paints
- ❖ Permanent markers
- ❖ Stickers
- ❖ Crayons

Finally, place a laminate (found in local craft stores) over both sides of the finished placemat. You want to make sure that everything is covered because you don't want kitty to accidentally chew or swallow decorations.

Cat Nap Bed

Kitty needs a cuddly place to sleep, besides your bed! So you might want to make her a one-of-a-kind bed to suit her purrr-sonality. Here are some creative ideas for building your own cat nap bed.

What you need:

- 🐾 Large cardboard box
- 🐾 Scissors
- 🐾 Nontoxic glue
- 🐾 Fabric, foam, padding
- 🐾 Decorations (stickers, feathers, rhinestones)

What you do:

1. Cut the top off of a large cardboard box so that it reaches about 4-6 inches (10-15 cm) high. Also cut a small space for your kitty to walk through.

2. Place padding for your cat to lay on inside the box—this can be fabric, foam, or another kind of padding. (You can even use an old pillowcase.) To secure the padding to the box, line it with nontoxic glue.

3. Choose a fabric to place on the outside of the box. (This can be a fun pattern, your cat's favorite colors, or decorated to match the room.) Use glue to affix the fabric around the box.

4. Line the inside or edges of the bed with different kinds of fabrics using glue. If your kitty has a wild side, she might like leopard-print or faux fur. A romantic kitty may prefer pink tulle or dark velvet.

5. For the final touches, add some cute decorations that bring out your cat's personality: spell out her name with rhinestones or affix some fun feathers with nontoxic glue.

There you have it! Now kitty's got her very own couture cat bed. What a sleeping beauty!

Many cats need to get used to places they meet for the first time—whether it's a cat carrier, home, or new bed. Try placing some of her fave toys inside the first time she uses something you make, or let her rub her hair against it—this will let kitty know that it's her special territory.

What Will You Make?

Kitty-licious Treats

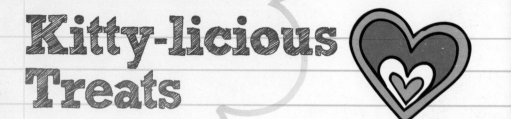

Your cat might not need a buffet of food to feel pampered, but a few delicious treats should do the trick!

This soothing "tea" meant for your cat will surely hit the spot!

What you need:

❀ 1 c. (237 ml) warm water

❀ 2 tbsp. (30 ml) catnip (fresh or dried)

❀ Bottle with cap

> Not all cats are crazy for catnip! Cats are actually born with a gene that reacts to it, so if your cat is born without that gene, don't expect her to go cuckoo for catnip. A taste for catnip may not develop until a kitten grows up.

What you do:

1. Place the catnip in a bottle (a small, empty water bottle should do).

2. Pour in warm water. Seal the cap tightly on the bottle.

3. Shake until the "tea" turns a green color.

Yum, now it's ready to serve to kitty! Serve to her in a pretty teacup (with an adult's permission) or a shallow bowl.

Purr-fect Popsicles

Whip up a batch of these snacks for your furry friend!

Your cat wants a taste of the good life! On a warm day, how about giving kitty an icy treat? This is a fun, easy recipe for making tuna-sicles for your furry friend.

What You Need:

❀ Can of tuna packed in water
❀ Mini ice cube tray

What you do:

1. Drain the liquid from canned tuna into the mini ice cube tray.
2. Place in freezer overnight.

Feed only two tuna cubes to your cat at one time—you don't want to overdo it! That's all there is to it! Now your kitty's got some tasty treats to help her cool off.

CAT CAKES

It's party time! Your cat wants some goodies from the "bakery," too. So try this recipe for cat cupcakes.

What you need:

- 3 baby carrots
- 12 oz. (375 g) canned tuna in water
- 3.75 oz. (106 g) cooked sardines in water
- 2 tbsp. (30 ml) bread crumbs
- 3 tbsp. (45 ml) grated parmesan cheese
- 1 tsp. (5 ml) catnip
- 1 egg beaten with a few pinches of bonito flakes and catnip for garnish (optional)
- Cupcake cups (the metal ones work best)

WARNING: You need an adult's supervision for this recipe.

What you do:

1. Preheat oven to 350 degrees F. In a plastic container, cook baby carrots with some water inside a microwave for 5 minutes or until they are soft. Drain and mash the carrots.

2. Drain tuna and sardines from the can. Reserve the liquid for use later (as garnish).

3. Combine all the ingredients and mix evenly (except the garnishes).

4. Now, you can either roll them up into balls or cook them inside molds. I used cupcake molds and fish molds. Bake for about 20 minutes or until they are firm. Let them cool completely before serving.

5. Sprinkle a bit of catnip and bonito flakes onto each cupcake. Drizzle with a bit of the tuna and sardine juice. Your kitty will LOVE it!

WARNING: Remember these are just treats! Kitty shouldn't have these all the time.

Cat Purr-sonalities

Cats, just like your friends, have different personalities that make them unique and special. A cat's personality can depend on a lot of factors, like age, breed, and genetics. But there are still some categories that most cats fall into. So check them out! What kind of personality does your cat have?

Real Party Animals

These cats tend to have big personalities and really stand out from the crowd. They like to be the center of attention and have a good time. This kitty usually entertains himself (or you!) with his wild antics and can be overflowing with confidence. They have tons of energy, which they use up just before it's time for a quick cat nap.

All About Love

Some cats get very affectionate, and that's what you'll find in this category. For the kitties that love to lie on your lap, purr, and massage you with their paws, you've found just the type who need nothing more than to give and receive love. Even if they don't show it all the time, these little Romeo and Juliet cats will come around on their own to show how much they care. For these kitties, who needs playtime when you've got lots of love?

Kitties Keepin' Busy

These little ones work really hard to help out—whether they're busy watching out the window, investigating inside bags or boxes, guarding the room from a high ledge, or following you from room to room (you've always wanted a bodyguard, right?). Hey, they just want to help out—even if that means playing with your pen or pouncing on your keyboard while you're doing homework!

Those Chatty Cats

Your cat is really saying things all the time. Do you know what her body language wants others to know? From the tip of her tail to her pointy ears, your cat's really got a lot to tell you!

Happy: When her tail is raised high in the hair, your cat must be in a happy mood. That probably happens around dinnertime or when it's time for a treat!

Afraid: Tucking the tail between the legs means that your cat is frightened by something.

Annoyed: Your kitty may swish her tail back and forth when she's feeling bothered. When her tail waves faster, that's a warning sign that she'd like to be left alone for a while.

Stop it!: If she paws at you (like when you're petting her), it probably means she'd like you to stop. That could be her way of telling you she's had enough for now.

Excited: A cat who's feeling curious or excited will twitch her tail, especially when she's on the prowl or about to pounce on a toy.

Exotic Cats

Black cats may cross your path all the time, but what about ones that look like little leopards or tigers? Some of the most beautiful breeds look just like wild cats, but are as domestic as calicos or tabbies. Here are a few exotic breeds, looking like they came right out of the jungle!

And remember, when it comes to these breeds, they might have very "wild" taste in fashion!

Some of the most popular cats we know of also include lions, tigers, leopards, and jaguars. You probably know about some of the other wild cats out there like cougars and cheetahs. Even these ferocious felines are similar to your little kitty in many ways! Just take a look at the different traits of your cat—the fur, teeth, or way of walking. Do any of these look like something a bigger wild cat might have?

Savannahs: Savannahs are very intelligent cats that like to be active. You might see them doing acrobatic stunts—leaping around like they're doing gymnastics! These pets look so exotic because they have an African wild cat called a Serval for an ancestor.

Bengals: These domestic cats come from the Asian Leopard Cat. Bengals are very affectionate and show a lot of devotion to their owners. They love to be part of the family.

Serengetis: Serengeti kitties are a mixture of Bengals with Oriental Shorthairs. Just like Savannahs, they are very playful when it comes to doing stunts. They like to be active and show off. Once they fit into a new home, they'll stick to you like glue.

Water Lovers: Not all cats enjoy the water, but did you know that some of them are very good swimmers? Bengals really like the water and sometimes splash around in their water bowls for entertainment. Another popular water-loving kitty is the Turkish Van, who may be found swishing around water from the faucet, toilet, or even your bath!

A Healthy Kitty Lifestyle

Cats are famous for having nine lives! So it's very important to take good care of your kitten so that she grows up to be healthy and happy. There are many things you can do as a loving pet owner to give your best feline friend a long, luxurious life.

Life in Kitty Years

You know how old your cat is in cat years, but what about human years? Is she still a baby, a teenager, or mature for her age? Check out this chart to find out how your cat compares! If you were a cat, how old would you be?

Cat Years	Human Years
6 months	10 years
1 year	15 years
3 years	28 years
5 years	36 years
7 years	44 years
9 years	52 years
11 years	60 years
13 years	69 years
15 years	76 years

Vet Visits

Caring for you kitten begins with vet visits from a very early age. You will want to ask a veterinarian for advice on how to feed your cat, what vaccinations might be needed, and how to look for signs that he or she might be sick.

Vet visits are much-needed checkups for your cat! It's important for you to keep an eye on your kitty's behavior, but pet doctors will take especially good notice of all the things you might normally miss, like fleas on the coat or mites in the ear. At the first sign of these icky creatures, let your vet know so the problem can be taken care of right away!

Do you have an indoor or outdoor cat? It's important for your vet to know! If your kitty likes to roam outdoors, he or she will need more vaccines than an indoor cat. These vaccines will help your cat stay healthy in the long run.

Equipment Needed to Care for Your Cat

Some cats are purr-fectly happy being independent, while others would much rather have all your attention. But no matter what, your cat still depends on you for being taken care of! Kitty will need certain supplies to be treated like a royal pet.

Collar and tag: Whether your cat is indoors or outdoors, you will want to have a collar and tag to ID her, just in case.

Grooming kit: You'll want to have grooming essentials for kitty, including the right brush, special shampoo, and other supplies that a vet can help you with.

Cat bed: Your precious one will need her beauty sleep! A comfy bed for her to take her fave cat naps on will ensure she's getting all the rest she needs.

Pet carrier: Very important! Whenever kitty goes on a trip or to the vet's, she'll need to be taken in a cat carrier.

Litterbox: You can find different litterbox sizes, depending on whether your kitty is big or small, or even the number of cats you have. You'll need certain supplies to help clean it out, too! (Too bad kitty can't help you with that!)

Food and water bowls

Toys: Toys are more than just fun for your cat; they help to keep his mind and body active! Toys are good for both mental and physical exercise.

Scratching post: These keep kitty from scratching up the furniture, where they mark their territory.

How to Keep a Healthy, Happy Cat

Kittens are busy creatures and need water to keep hydrated. With all of that running and leaping around, make sure that your feline always has access to fresh water.

Some cats would rather drink running water, so a fountain (available in pet stores) might be a good idea for these choosy cats.

Feeding Time!

Mealtime for kitty is very important— a healthy diet makes for a happy cat! Even if he is super picky about supper, it's still important that your feline friend eats the right food.

Their dinner should be made of half meat, half veggies, which you can get from ready-made cat food in stores. They'll need a good mix of both wet and dry food. But if you only give dry food, be sure to also provide plenty of water!

The Kitty Life

Grooming

You probably know that your cat takes very good care of herself when it comes to grooming, especially grooming her fur. But when you groom your cat it creates a great bonding experience!

Some benefits include:

- Spending quality time together
- Checking for fleas or parasites
- Minimizing hairballs and knots
- Removing dead hairs
- Spreading organic oils on your cat's coat
- Improving muscle tone
- Stimulating blood circulation
- Keeping fur off the furniture
- Making your cat feel extra-loved with attention

Depending on hair length, cats need different types of brushes.

If your cat's having a bad day and doesn't want brushing, try calming her with soft strokes and a soothing voice. You can offer her a treat for distraction while you start to groom her.

Shorthairs:

Use a fine-tooth comb as well as a natural bristle once a week. This removes unwanted hairs.

Longhairs: Use a steel comb once a day.

The best way to comb kitty's hair is to stroke gently down in the direction of fur growth. When using the bristle brush, very lightly stroke up toward the head, then downward again. (This removes dead hairs from kitty's coat.) If kitty's hair is matted, tease out knots with your fingers or ask an adult to clip them with nonpointed scissors.

Smell-Good Kitty Litter

If you don't clean out your kitty litter on a regular basis, it'll start to stink pretty soon. Your kitty also likes for her litter to smell fresh, so why not add some nice scent to make her feel pampered?

What you do: Combine 16 oz. of baking soda with 4 tsp. (20 ml) of dried mint. Stir together very well, and then add to your kitty's litterbox. This is only for her litterbox, not for eating!

Cat Crossing!

Solve the crossword puzzle to match kitty clues to their right answers.

(Hint: All clues relate to facts found throughout this book!)

ACROSS

1. Kitty may have several of these in one day because she needs her beauty sleep (2 words)
4. These go securely around your cat's neck to make her identifiable and can also be a fun decoration (3 words)
6. Tamed cats that are no longer wild
9. Ballet move meaning the "step of cat," which leaps to the side (3 words)
10. Herb that many cats receive as a treat
11. A crucial part of your cat's diet, because she's a carnivore
12. Name given to sacred cats in Ancient Egypt
13. Ancient culture that worshipped cats and used them to scare away pests
14. This must-have equipment will get very smelly and icky if you don't clean it often
16. A thick, double-coated fur (as opposed to short- or longhair)
17. What your cat does to her fur everyday
18. This grooming tool will help you smooth kitty's hair and check for fleas or other parasites
19. A special pet doctor who will help make sure your cat is healthy

DOWN

2. A tiny creature (like a flea) that can live on your cat
3. Cat breeds very similar in appearance and nature to wild cats
5. Fun objects to play with that also keep kitty physically and mentally exercised
7. Usually covered with fabric or rope, these objects give kitty a safe place to scrape their claws (2 words)
8. Pilgrim ship that first arrived in the U.S., bringing the first American cats
9. Use this to tote your feline friend around town or to the vet's office (2 words)
15. When your cat rubs against you, she's really "marking" this

Can You Spot the Differences?

Take a good look at the pictures of these two spotted cats. Can you tell what's different between them?

A.

B.

Cat IQ

Test out your cat knowledge in this true or false quiz:

1. **True or false?**

   Cats of all kinds walk on their toes.

2. **True or false?**

   Your cat rubs against you (or the couch or chair!) to let you know when he feels hungry.

3. **True or false?**

   Just like your housecat, lions and tigers purr when they feel affectionate.

4. **True or false?**

   Your playful pet pounces on toy mice and wads of paper in the same way that big cats pounce on prey to have for dinner.

5. **True or false?**

   Sometimes your kitty wakes up during the night and goofs around because he actually doesn't like the dark.

Kitty Word Search

All the breeds of cats got mixed up in the pet store! Can you help search for them? You'll find them diagonally, backward, forward, sideways, and up and down.

Word List:

Abyssinian

American Bobtail

Balinese

Bengal

Bombay

Burmese

Chartreux

Cornish Rex

Devon Rex

Dragon Li

Egyptian Mau

Exotic Shorthair

Havana Brown

Javanese

Maine Coon

Manx

Ragamuffin

Russian Blue

Savannah

Siamese

Singapura

Tonkinese

Turkish Van

```
r e s e n a v a j b o m b a y
l i a t b o b n a c i r e m a
s s a i l n o g a r d h a b n
a i u h c w d c w b e n g a l
v a n b t o s e e b x e i l u
a m i n s r r b v n r n b i a
n e f s a b o n h o i a u n m
n s f e i a o h i s n a r e n
a e u l b n a i s s u r m s a
h n m v e a g y a c h s e e i
e i a r s v b a h a i r s x t
v k g t n a o i p a t t e n p
g n a c n h l n n u i a o x y
a o r o m c h a r t r e u x g
y t u r k i s h v a n a a g e
```

67

A Hidden Meow-ssage!

Your cat wants you to know something very special. Find the three words in the puzzle below (diagonally, up, down, sideways, backward, or forward), and cross them out. The letters left over will spell out a message to you about kitties.

BICOLOR　　　**CALICO**　　　**STRIPES**

R	O	L	O	C	I	B
T	I	M	C	E	S	P
S	T	R	I	P	E	S
E	N	T	L	W	I	T
H	C	A	A	T	S	I
S	N	E	C	V	E	R
W	A	S	T	E	D	M

__ __ __ __ __

__ __ __ __ __

__ __ __ __

__ __ __ __

__ __ __

__ __ __ __

__ __ __ __ __.

An A-maze-ing Cat!

Uh-oh! Kitty really wants to play with the ball of yarn, but she can't reach it from where she is! Help her get through the maze so she can unravel some fun.

START

FINISH

Pretty as a Picture!

*You know your cat pretty well by now.
Draw her doing some of her favorite things!*

If kitty could go anywhere, where would it be? Draw kitty hanging out there!

Draw a picture of you and your kitty together.

What's kitty's favorite thing to do?

Draw a pic of kitty eating his or her fave food.

Which Cat Said That?

Match the quote to the famous kitty who said it.
For an extra challenge, match them to real-life
photos of the look-a-like kitties!

COLUMN 1

1. "Why, we can have lots of good fun, if you wish..."

2. "Deep down inside, we're all cats, right?"

3. "Fear me if you dare! Hissss!"

4. "You may have noticed that I'm not all there myself."

5. "Oh no! I overslept! I'm late! For my nap."

6. "Cats rule and dogs drool."

7. "No mouse is no match for no cat. And I'm a cat. I think. MEOW! Yep, I'm a cat."

8. "Dogs guard; cats watch...and judge."

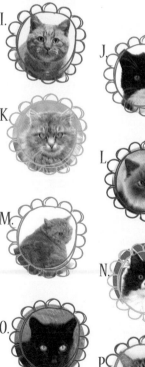

COLUMN 2

A.   Garfield *(Garfield)*

B.   Salem *(Sabrina, the Teenage Witch)*

C.   Milo *(Milo and Otis)*

D.   Cat in the Hat *(The Cat in the Hat)*

E.   Sassy *(Homeward Bound: The Incredible Journey)*

F.   Sylvester the Cat *(Sylvester and Tweety)*

G.   Cheshire Cat *(Alice in Wonderland)*

H.   Puss in Boots *(Shrek movies)*

COLUMN 3

I.

J.

K.

L.

M.

N.

O.

P.

The Kitty Gallery

BFF

This section offers a special place for you to keep memories of your favorite feline! You can paste photos, fill with stickers, write poems, draw pictures, or make up stories about your cat.

CAT
Gallery

COOL

Say Cheese!

Wow!

Answers to Puzzles and Games

Page 63: Cat Crossing!

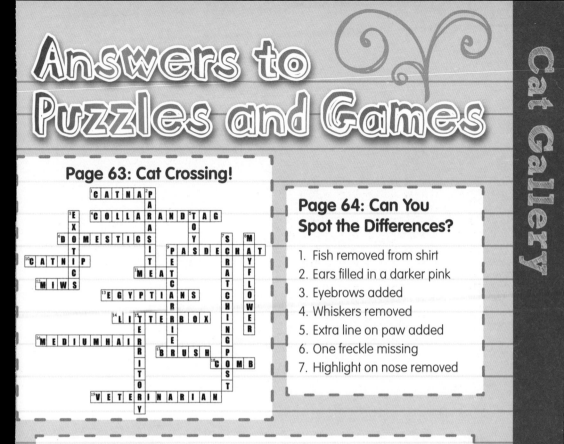

				¹C	A	T	N	A	²P										
									A										
	³E		⁴C	O	L	L	A	R	A	N	D	⁵T	A	G					
	X								A			O							
⁶D	O	M	E	S	T	I	C	S				Y		⁷S		⁸M			
	T							I		⁹P	A	S	D	E	C	H	A	T	
¹⁰C	A	T	N	I	P			T				E		R		Y			
	C						¹¹M	E	A	T		C		A		F			
¹²M	I	W	S					C				R		T		L			
				¹³E	G	Y	P	T	I	A	N	S		C		O			
								R						H		W			
		¹⁴L	¹⁵I	T	T	E	R	B	O	X			I		E			
			E											N		R			
¹⁶M	E	D	I	U	M	H	A	I	R					G					
			R			¹⁷B	R	U	S	H				P					
			I							¹⁸C	O	M	B					
			T										S						
			O										T						
		¹⁹V	E	T	E	R	I	N	A	R	I	A	N						

Page 64: Can You Spot the Differences?

1. Fish removed from shirt
2. Ears filled in a darker pink
3. Eyebrows added
4. Whiskers removed
5. Extra line on paw added
6. One freckle missing
7. Highlight on nose removed

Page 65: Cat IQ

1. **True.** Their toes have soft pads that protect their foot bones while running and jumping around. It also helps big and small cats to walk quietly—so they can sneak up more easily when no one's looking!

2. **False.** Cats rub up against you and other objects in your house because, just like tigers rub against a tree, they are marking their territory. They're saying, "This one's all mine!"

3. **False.** While your cat's sounds may sometimes seem like a purring machine, his bigger cousins don't have the ability to purr. Their vocal cords are attached differently to the skull, so they make very different sounds.

4. **True.** All types of cats like to stalk and hunt their food. It's a natural instinct for them to sneak up and quickly strike at objects—usually pinning them down with their paws and claws.

5. **False.** Most cats are nocturnal creatures, meaning that they naturally have an active nightlife. Your kitty—just like wild cats—has excellent hearing and eyesight for being busy and staying alert in the dark.

Page 67: Kitty Word Search

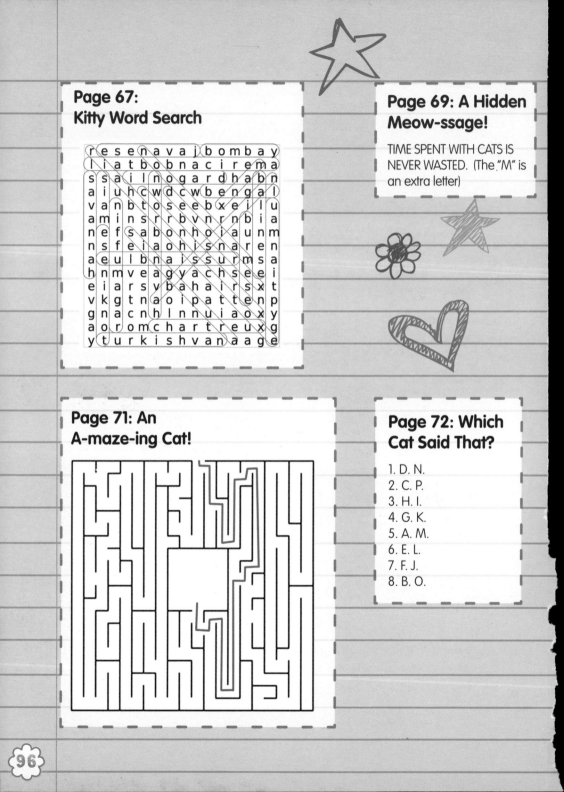

```
r e s e n a v a j b o m b a y
l i a t b o b n a c i r e m a
s s a i l n o g a r d h a b n
a i u h c w d c w b e n g a l
v a n b t o s e e b x e i l u
a m i n s r r b v n r n b i a
n e f s a b o n h o i a u n m
n s f e i a o h i s n a r e n
a e u l b n a i s s u r m s a
h n m v e a g y a c h s e e i
e i a r s y b a h a i r s x t
v k g t n a o i p a t t e n p
g n a c n h l n n u i a o x y
a o r o m c h a r t r e u x g
y t u r k i s h v a n a a g e
```

Page 69: A Hidden Meow-ssage!

TIME SPENT WITH CATS IS NEVER WASTED. (The "M" is an extra letter)

Page 71: An A-maze-ing Cat!

Page 72: Which Cat Said That?

1. D. N.
2. C. P.
3. H. I.
4. G. K.
5. A. M.
6. E. L.
7. F. J.
8. B. O.